# Dear Celebrity

## One Woman's Search
## For
## Love Among the Stars

By
Traci E. Langston

# Dedication

This book is dedicated to a variety of individuals. Of course, my friends who put up with all the strangeness from me and enjoyed the responses. Tom T. who provided me with the addresses of the celebrities and without whom none of this would have been possible. And finally, those special men who distracted me from my purpose and made my feelings run deeper than I expected. They are truly remarkable men. Although the feelings were not mutual, they will always be special.

# Preface

"This may seem like a very odd letter on the outset, but I assure you that it's honest." That is how it started. All of this began with one letter. A letter to a comedian who got his own show. Then I bought a celebrity address list. I wrote some more. I used the same letter. Again, and again and again. A photocopied letter sent to dozens of men. I won't disclose the exact vast numbers because it would cause those who did not receive the letter to feel left out. Suffice it to say, that I spent a lot of money on postage over the years of researching this book.

The letter was not a standard fan letter. In fact, it wasn't a true fan letter at all. I did not make reference to their work. I couldn't due to the fact that it had to be a very general letter. I said I was attracted to them as a person.

It is not unusual for a person to reach out to a celebrity. It is an unusual case when that celebrity reaches back. What could prompt such behavior? And how far would this contact go?

When a civilian crosses paths with a celebrity, it is almost a dance similar to that of a sword fight. The parry and thrust of approach and retreat. The celebrity is immediately on the defensive while the civilian is in the role of the aggressor. On the rare occasion that both parties drop their defenses and approach one another as equals and real human beings is when true understanding of each other occurs.

I understand the world of celebrity much better now. It is complex and challenging and, at times, lonely. I thank all the men who let me into their world.

This process took a long time to complete. Some of my statements and activities may seem dated because of this. I also may jump back and forth between past and present tense of my phrasing. It's all in the past but writing this has helped me relive these wonderful experiences again.

# Introduction

This entire process began as a farce. I was bored at work. I purchased a celebrity address list. I wrote a form letter. I mailed a lot of letters. Then I waited.

I wanted to know if a letter that was not essentially a "fan" letter would get a response. I did not request a photo or an autograph. I was sending a letter of introduction and interest.

The shock was that I did get responses and the extent of the responses that I received. Why would a celebrity call a total stranger? Why would they give out their home phone number? What did they hope to achieve? Due to some of the responses, they hoped to achieve sex. The largest response was to appease a little fan who is in awe of a great star. A few seemed genuinely lonely in their lives and would like a friend.

No matter what the reason or response, the process was fun and I enjoyed it a lot. I am thankful to all the celebrities who were unknowing guinea pigs in this study. I have not used names or specifics to protect the identities of those celebrities who did respond.

# Back Story

Several years ago, there was a comic who had his own TV show. This has become a fairly common occurrence. I enjoyed the show for its brief run. The star was a man that I found attractive. He was my type (if I even have a type).

One night I was eating dinner and watching the show. Then the idea hit me: why not write him a letter? He could ignore it or not. I wrote the letter.

After the series of events, I wrote an article about it and submitted it to several magazines. No one wanted it. By this point the show had been cancelled and he had slipped back into the comedy club circuit. Perhaps he wasn't big enough. I include the article here to show the evolution of celebrity contact.

After this I realized that if he answered who else might? If I had seen my article published, none of this might have happened. I would have merely been happy with my success. Probably not though. Why settle for a grain of sand when there is an entire beach in front of you?

# Dear Jack

"This may seem like a very odd letter on the outset, but I assure you it's honest."

That's how it all started. I was bored and watching TV. A sitcom was on. I decided to see what sort of response a fan letter would get. Jack was cute and had a new show on NBC. I figured, "why not?" So off went a letter to Jack's production company. Then I waited.

I didn't have to wait long. Less than two weeks later, I got a big envelope with a return address of only "Hollywood." I opened my mail to see Jack's face smiling out at me. He had also included a cast photo. Both were signed and had a brief note about my "grooviness." I compared the writing, the signature and the envelope and decided that all three had been written by the same person. Either Jack had done this or there was a very busy assistant forging Jack's signature.

I took this as a sign of encouragement. I wrote back. Etiquette requires a thank you note for all gifts received. These photos were gifts. So, off went another letter to Jack. Again, I waited. Once more I was not disappointed. A quick reply was forthcoming.

One day I find a large envelope in my mail and once again it bore the now familiar return address of "Hollywood." I opened the envelope and was pleasantly surprised. Whereas the first enveloped contained a cast photo and an individual photo of Jack in character, this one held a photo of Jack as a potential movie star. It was a glossy look stud-muffin picture. This was Jack as Jack. No smile, soft hair and an intense look. Eyes you lose normally behind the hair and the grin, now gazed seductively from a black and white photo.

It got better and better. There was a note attached. A semi-personal one that said he thought he had already answered this letter, but if not, to enjoy another picture. Granted, there had yet to be any reference to anything that I had written so it was highly possible that my address was merely added to a list and my correspondence discarded. However, I had received another gift and this required a thank you.

So off goes another letter. At this point I am seeing images of restraining orders so I decided that I would not write again without a sign. Some spiritual guide clocked in some overtime because me sign came; and on my birthday no less.

As I was flipping through the paper looking for amusing entertainment for my celebration, I saw Jack's face smiling out at me. He was to appear at the Improv the weekend of my birthday. Good sign. I called and left a message at the Improv to let Jack know I had called. In my last letter, I had promised to take him for coffee or drinks if he ever came to my city. Well here he was and it was very rude to ignore your promises. Miss Manners would be so proud of me.

My message stated only that I needed another fuzzy horse. On the second envelope from Jack, there was a sticker of a horse. It was fuzzy. I found this odd from an adult man. Mostly it was quirky. I found it fun and amusing. I had made reference to it in my last letter. It also had a personal feel to a message left at the comedy club. I left my name and number as well. Alas, Jack did not call. Granted I was gone a lot during the weekend and he may not like to leave messages on machines. Besides, what do you say to a girl you have never met? There was only one alternative: go see Jack.

As part of my polite thank you's, I had returned the photo favor by sending a picture of myself to Jack. I figured it was only fair and the right thing to do. So, if Jack had ever seen my letters, he would know what I looked like.

I was seated in the front row of tables. In fact, I leaned on the stage. My gaze rarely left Jack. I figured if he looked at the audience, I had a chance of being seen. Now, he could be one of those performers that will look at their audience and never really see them. If he is not, then he saw me. In fact, he looked directly at me. I'm not sure if I saw any recognition or that he merely noticed me as an attractive woman.

I never did talk to Jack that evening. Yes, he was in the lobby after the show. Yes, all I needed to do was walk up to him. But he was turned away from the exiting crowd and talking with someone. And after all, when push comes to shove, I am incredibly shy and insecure. I walked past him and went home.

Perhaps it was for the best. Jack had mentioned a girlfriend in his act. I hope she really does exist and they are happy. Jack lives in California. I live hundreds of miles away. Jack is a performer and I have been burned by them before. Jack believes in commitment, I am a commitment-phobe. I am kind, pretty, intelligent, fun and ambitious. I have been called the perfect woman by more than one man. So, Jack, maybe it is best that we never met. Let us live with the memories of what almost was. In the end, I would have only broken your heart.

# The Letter

This may seem like a very odd letter on the outset, but I assure you it's honest.

Unfortunately, due to your career, this is how I first noticed you. If I had seen you at a party or in a bar, I could have merely approached you and spoken.

Granted, I don't know all that much about you. So, no weird declarations of love and plans of forever. For all I know, you could be a real jerk. I find you attractive on a variety of levels and would like to get to know you. Who knows, maybe at a later point I'll ask permission to court you. (I am an old-fashioned liberated woman.)

Before you decide I'm a crackpot, let me tell you about myself. I am a 30 year old woman. I have a degree in theatre from Arizona State University. I've worked in the film and television industry for 10 years. (See, I'm not a lonely housewife on a farm in Iowa.) I understand strange lives and schedules.

I'm ½ Native American. I have a slightly exotic look. I've even been called beautiful on occasion (by people outside my family). I have brown hair which almost reaches my waist. I have high cheekbones and good skin. My eyes are hazel with flecks of gold. I am 5'6" with a good figure.

I enjoy art, music, reading and of course film and theatre. My great passions are the environment, crime and disease. The future of the world is our responsibility. I belong to no organized religion. I celebrate Christmas but more for the sense of love and family with the spirit of giving. I adore Halloween. I believe in ghosts.

That's me. Who are you? Feel free to write or call anytime. You could have a new friend if nothing else.

# The Follow Up Letter

Not everyone responded to the initial letter so I sent a second letter to those celebrities that I really did want to meet. Of course, this list was much smaller so I made the letter more detailed.

Hi Again!

Yes, I have written you before but never got a response. Maybe you never got the letter or it just didn't spark your interest. Don't worry, I am not some kind of psycho or anything.

I know that you hear this a lot but I find you very attractive. Of course, that doesn't mean anything really. I am not a superficial person. A man could be the most beautiful example of the human form ever but then he opens his mouth and you discover an idiot beyond compare. I am hoping that is not the case with you.
This feels weird because it's not a true fan letter. It is more of a personal ad with only one reader.

So now the description of me. I am 33 years old, 5'6" tall, brown hair, hazel eyes. No, that sounds way too drab. How's this: A young woman with an attractive figure, long hair the color of honey-coated copper and almond eyes of sage and brown. With skin of sun-kissed olive tones and high cheekbones, I have an exotic look accented with a warm smile and inviting lips.

So now you can take your pick as to which you prefer, the sterile or the poetic. That covered the looks area. I am hoping you are not a person who judges solely on appearance so you would want a bit about me as a person. I enjoy reading, listening to music (anything but rap or twangy country), gardening, movies, nature and travel (I have been to all 50 states). I cook (specifically baking and French), I write (I am working on my first novel) and I sing and dance (alone in my home).

At about this point in the letter you are most likely saying "this woman has everything I have ever been looking for in a person." Sorry, not everything. I do not have a yacht or a mansion on the Riviera. I have never been to Europe. But those are merely material possessions. Yes, I was a debutante and learned tennis and golf at the family's country club. I enjoy polo matches, true, but I also bowl. I am a study in contrasts.

My favorite color is black. My favorite actress is Katherine Hepburn. Favorite poet: Emily Dickenson. Favorite dessert: (tie) hot fudge sundae & cheesecake. Favorite author: (tie) Edgar Allen Poe & Charles Dickens. Favorite singer: Barry Manilow. Favorite painter: Claude Monet (2nd is Renoir). Favorite modern painter: Keith Haring (2nd is Andy Warhol).

Turn ons: Zoos, the circus, cats, the ocean, good food, learning.

Turn offs: War, racism, environmental crimes, selfish politicians, people who refuse to learn, illiteracy.

If I were stranded on a desert island the one book I would want with me: The Oxford English Dictionary.

I hope that you have enjoyed this letter. I hope that your interest has been sparked.

# Brian

Brian was in his mid-50's, divorced and has children. He is an actor and has had a successful television career. He is from the middle section of America originally. He shares custody of his children. He's active (he jogs in the evenings). He lives in the Los Angeles area. He has dark hair. He owns a dog. He called me in response to my first letter and left his phone number.

I believe that Brian was surprised that he called me. He was wary to leave his phone number. He didn't quite understand why I wrote him. Still he called me several times. We had pleasant phone conversations. I really enjoyed getting to know him. We shared many interests. We talked about our lives. He spoke of his kids and his ex-wife. He told me a lot about himself. I was glad when I got a message from him. We had long talks all evening and brief ones before he had friends over for dinner. He would call me when he got in from his run. I looked forward to talking to him.

The end came when he could not get past the age difference of over 20 years. I was disappointed. I felt we had developed a friendship. I was truly attracted to him. He is a very good -looking man. He left the decision up to me. I could call if I wanted to pursue a relationship. He gave me time to think about it. I let it go because I knew it was something he was uncomfortable about. I stopped calling him.

When I worked in L.A., one job I had was as a production assistant. A duty befell me one day to go to an agency to get a picture of Brian. I drove around that day with his picture on the car seat next to me. I didn't leave it in the envelope. I wanted to look at it. His eyes are what get me. They hold a lot of depth.

I do miss Brian. I didn't expect to truly meet anyone. Especially someone that I was attracted to beforehand. I did lose my scientific perspective with him. I am glad he called. Getting to know him was a treat.

# Relatively Speaking

I sent the letter to several men who were related. Often brothers but occasionally a father and son. The pattern that emerged is that relatives are similar in their responses. One actor answered whose father is also an actor. I had not written to his father. He sent a personalized autographed picture.

I got a photo with a form note from a son of another actor. The lack of responses from the other leads me to wonder if as a family they decided not to respond to any fan mail or if it was a style of upbringing.

One pair of brothers had the same address for mailings. I sent each of them a letter and mailed them on the same day. I never heard from them. Toss into this mix the fact that I had met them before through industry events. The elder one and I used to work together, indirectly. I have had conversations with him. We have mutual friends. Our paths have crossed several times over the last few years. He is a nice guy. I have always found him attractive. His brother is okay but doesn't appeal to me the as his older brother does.

So I wonder if he ever saw the letter. Perhaps he saw his and showed his brother who had received the same letter. They may have had a good laugh at the audacity of someone to send a form letter to celebrities. They most likely do not remember me at all.

If they did see the letters, as with the other related men, why not respond or have an assistant respond? I didn't even get the standard picture with preprinted signature.

The set of brothers were in the most appropriate age category. They were all single or divorced. Close in age to myself. Yet none of them responded. It would have been interesting to see how men who are related and close in age respond to fans. I suppose the answer to that is: they don't.

# Walt

I sent my first letter to Walt with no response. So, Walt was a recipient of the second letter. From that letter, I received a phone call. He called from a recording studio as he finished up his latest album. I wasn't home so he left a funny message about me never being home and the number at the studio.

I got home late so it was the next day before I called the studio. Whoever answered asked if I was (insert woman's name here). I said no. He got embarrassed. Walt had finished recording and was gone. I left a message to let him know I had called. He didn't call again.

Over the next several months, I sent him my picture, a small gift and cards for his birthday, Christmas and Valentine's Day. They were very casual notes. Still he didn't call or write.

I sent a Christmas card and received one from him. Maybe it was from his office, sent by an assistant. It was something though.

One day, a friend called to tell me Walt was coming in concert. I sent off a card telling him we could meet for a drink when he was in my town. As with all my correspondence, I included my phone number. My friends and I got tickets for the show.

A couple of days before the show, I arranged for flowers to be sent to the theater for him. Again, my phone number was on the card. I was a nervous wreck. Walt was one that I was really attracted to. I had found him attractive since high school. He was a man I thought I could really enjoy spending time with. He was one of the men that started me thinking about the entire celebrity contact thing in the first place.

The day of the show I did my hair and makeup carefully. I wore a new shirt that showed off my figure. My friends encouraged me throughout the show. We laughed that there was no security checking for me with my photo. I had tried very hard to avoid any hint of stalker mentality.

The show was fantastic. I was thoroughly impressed with his energy and staging. A very talented man indeed.

After the show, we went down front and asked a security person to see if my flowers had arrived. I wanted to make sure that the flower shop did as I had paid them to do. The security man came back and said that Walt's dressing room door was closed so he didn't know. We told him my name and he said for us to wait outside by the stage door.

We went outside and joined a crowd of about 100 fans. I used my friend's cell phone to check my messages. There were no messages from Walt. We waited. We talked about my contact so far with Walt. Some of the fans around us were looking at me oddly.

Then the fates smiled. The security man came out and yelled my name. I waved and he said, "You're kidding." I told him no and offered ID. He said "Come on. Walt wants to see you." I left my friends and was led backstage. He told me Walt had been on the phone calling me when they told him I was there. I was led downstairs to a door. A brief image of crazed rock stars attacking fans for sex in their dressing rooms crossed my mind. I silently hoped that the security guard would stay outside the door. He knocked, opened the door, I walked in, the door closed and I was alone and face to face with Walt.

He was sitting casually in a chair. He offered me a seat. I sat on the sofa across from him. He offered me some food from the fruit tray or something to drink. I looked at a strawberry and wondered how seductively I could eat one. I decided I couldn't and declined the offer of food. He nibbled on honeydew melon. I found it highly enticing and erotic. We chatted about a variety of things.

He picked up the stake that held the card in the flowers I sent. He fidgeted with it while we spoke. The flowers were nowhere to be seen. They were either on the bus or in the trash.

He told me that he had been on the phone calling me when they told him I was there. He told me I had been on the backstage list. He had no idea about me or what type of person I was other than from a few cards and letters. Yet he was calling me, put me on the backstage list and was alone with me in his dressing room.

I had a purse with me. I passed through no metal detectors and was not searched. He opened himself up for anything. Sure, I look normal, but one never knows.

After about 15 minutes, he had to go out and sign autographs. He had just finished his show when he thought to call me. Then he made all those people wait while we spoke. It made me feel pretty special. He gave me a hug as I was leaving.

I went back outside and waited with my friends. Walt came out and signed autographs for every person there. He was kind and patient. My friends and I got in line. He smiled and said "hi there" when he saw me. I handed him the Christmas card I got from him. A brief look I can't describe crossed his face. Perhaps it was from seeing the Christmas card. Perhaps it was the fact that I was getting an autograph. I had changed into a fan. He signed the card and the tickets of my friends. I put my hand out to shake his and thank him. He took my hand in both of his and smiled. It was a very warm smile.

Walt is a very special person to me now. When he performs, he has a very definite stage persona. However, in the dressing room I met the man, not the personality. That was a very special man. He was very attractive, kind and the perfect gentleman.

I know that during this experiment and research, I was opening myself up to all sorts of possibilities. One thing I didn't count on was finding a man that shook me up and made me want more. When we spoke, I felt as though I was on a first date. I was very nervous. I got distracted by his warm and expressing eyes, his genuine smile and honest caring.

I've heard stories of couples that see each other and know they have found the one. They usually tell these stories on their golden wedding anniversary. I always dismissed these stories as romantic hogwash. Then I met Walt. I knew that if I spoke with him again, I may lose my heart entirely.

# Roger

Roger was in his mid-50s, divorced and has children. He is an actor and has had a successful television career. He is from the middle section of America originally. He shares custody of his children. He's active (scuba dives). He lives in the Los Angeles area. He has dark hair. He owns a dog. He called me in response to my first letter and left his phone number.

Roger and I spoke for over an hour during our first conversation. He asked me when I was planning a trip to Los Angeles so he could meet me face to face. He also asked me more personal questions as well. I think the information regarding my bust size may have disappointed him. Well, he did ask.

He called me several times. I was free to call him. We spoke several times. He is a nice man who has a good sense of humor. He obviously has a strong sense of adventure as well. He has a pilot's license. He was always very friendly when we talked. We discussed my life, his life, his kids and his dog. We spoke of lives, not careers.

Roger was fun. At some point, he lost interest. I am not sure why. Perhaps he became bored. Perhaps because I am a Republican and he is a Democrat. Maybe he didn't like the birthday card I sent him. I will never know for sure.

# On The Subject of Race

The letter went out to men without regard to ethnic background. As I am a woman of mixed heritage, I felt no need to curtail my attentions to one racial group. Anglo, Asian, African American, Latino, and American Indian were all sent letters. Due to the patterns of the entertainment industry, the majority of performers were white.

I received two responses from minority actors. One was from an Asian actor. He sent a picture with my name and a real signature. The other was a picture with a preprinted signature from a black actor/director. One could argue that the ratio of percentages of letters sent to responses received was well balanced by this response.

One very prominent black actor did not send anything. I expected at least a picture because he is reported as being very nice. Granted, my letter never requested a photo or fan club information. Taken at face value, he should not have responded to my letter. If he did, his wife would most likely be rather upset. As she should be.

We often hear of the struggles of minorities in the entertainment industry. There are reports of minorities working harder for the same recognition. My letter could be seen as recognition. The majority did not even send pictures or fan club information.

# Nick

Nick is in his mid-50s, divorced and has children. He is an actor and has had a successful television career. His children are grown. He lives in New York. He has dark hair. He called me in response to my second letter and left his pager number.

Nick was thoroughly intrigued with why I wrote and tried to often to reach me. We spoke a few times. We talked about his work. We talked about his life. We talked about his children. We talked about him.

Nick is a very attractive man. He has what are often referred to as bedroom eyes. His voice is slow and seductive. He invites fantasies of soft music and candlelight. When he asked me if I was sexy, I wanted to scream "yes!" Instead I said I didn't know and turned the question on him. He said yes, because he is a very sexual person. Suffice it to say, he could make a girl melt into the floor.

Looks and a great voice can only go so far however. He never really seemed to want to know about me. He alluded to a girlfriend. He requested a photo of me. Apparently, he didn't like the way I looked. I haven't heard from him since.

# 1st Letter to Walt

It was a great pleasure to finally meet you face to face. I was pleased to discover that you are a polite and thoughtful man.

I was so nervous. I hope that I didn't make a complete fool of myself. As you discovered, I am rather shy in person. I wanted to make a good impression.

You made a very good impression on me. You work very hard during your show. This was the first I ever attended. You truly give your audience what they came for.

For me personally, when we were speaking in your dressing room, I was very distracted by your eyes. They are incredible. I would have liked to have gazed into them longer. You are a very attractive man. I had to look away occasionally to clear my mind.

So, again, I am glad we met finally. I do hope that you meant it when you said we could keep in touch. I would like to learn more about you and let you get to know me. As your schedule permits.

I was amazed at so much about you during and after the show. You are a giving, kind person. You will always have a friend in me.

# On The Subject Of Love

In the dedication of this book, I mentioned the fact that I had developed feelings beyond research. I tried to deny the fact to myself for a long time. Things happen that we really have no control over. This was true of Walt.

I had always heard those stories of couples who saw each other and just knew that was it. They tell you these stories in their old age after decades together. I am a romantic and felt that they were sweet stories but nothing like that happened in today's world. Boy, was I wrong. The minute I walked into that dressing room, it was like the earth dropped out from under me. I was lost and didn't want to come back.

Since that time, I noticed changes in my life. Men that held appeal for me before were not as interesting to me anymore. My dreams, thoughts and fantasies became filled with Walt. I consciously tried to fill my mind with other men. There didn't seem to be room anymore.

Now some of you are saying "She was just star struck." I wasn't. I've been in the entertainment industry for a lot of years. I have met celebrities galore. There are some that have been very pleasant people and some that are completely rude to everyone. Then there are the egomaniacs. It's just a job and they are just people. You get all types of personalities.

I have dated rich and poor, gorgeous and ugly. I've known stars and unknowns. There are award winners and yet-to-be's. Fame is a fleeting thing. When Andy Warhol said that we all have 15 minutes of fame, he wasn't far off.

My feelings weren't about fame or celebrity. I truly believe if he had been a regular person I met in a bar or at the office, he would had had the same effect on me.

# 2nd Letter to Walt

I remember the first time I saw you on MTV. There was something special about you. I was happy whenever I saw a new video. You showed a real joy for life.

Time passed and I would occasionally see a new video or hear something. You were still attractive. I found you alluring. Yes, I liked your music. I respected your vast talent. I was never what you would call a fan. I owned no albums. I didn't seek out information on you. I joined no clubs.

Then one day I saw you on television. All the things I found fascinating about you before were still there but with an added maturity. I decided I should toss caution to the wind and write you. I had no idea what would happen. I was just a woman trying to meet a man she found handsome.

I could scarcely believe it when you called. I am sorry that I didn't get back to you in time for us to talk. The cards and letters I sent after that were to see I there was any interest. There was nothing until this past Christmas when I received your card.

Then my friend called and told me about your concert. I attended the concert with several friends. They knew of my attraction to you. I told them that I had sent you flowers at the theater.

I was extremely surprised when you had me come backstage. It never occurred to me that I might be on the backstage list. I was very nervous when I got to your dressing room. You were so relaxed.

You are even more good looking in person. Your voice and manner are friendly and kind. Your eyes hold a warmth that I have never seen in anyone else. The situation had the feeling of a first date for me. Maybe I tried too hard, maybe not hard enough.

I knew that you only saw me as a fan and not a woman you could have been attracted to by a single response from you. I asked if there was anything that you wanted to know about me. You simply said "no." There was no interest from you.

I hope that you were happy to meet me, no matter how you see me. I was very happy to meet you. I don't regret any of the things that I did or the reasons I did them. I never will.

I don't know if you felt anything when we met. If you only see me as a fan, then you may have only thought I was nice. My situation is different. I don't look at you as a celebrity. I never have. I wanted to stay and talk with you when we met. I was fascinated. You seem to be a man I would enjoy learning more about.

I don't know if there is such a thing as love at first sight. If there is, this has got to be it. You made my head spin and my world turn upside down. You affected me to my very core. I don't know if I 'll ever fully recover. I don't know if I want to.

I am a kind, honest, intelligent, funny and interesting person. I am loyal to my friends and family. You will always have a place in my heart. A friend at the very least. Thank you for all that you have given me. You are a remarkable man who has truly enriched my life.

# Calling All Stars

The telephone is an amazing invention. And with the invention comes all of its modern accessories. A phone, an answering machine and caller ID. There's also last call return and more. I had all these fun gadgets and I am sure that many celebrities do too.

There were days I would return home and find my message light blinking with a call from an actor or musician. The machine gave me the date and time of the call. Last call return gave me a phone number on occasion. Then I got caller ID.

Walt called before I had caller ID. He had called from a recording studio. Smart move on his part. I got a number but not one that is exclusively his.

Nick did not realize apparently that none of his numbers are blocked. He unknowingly gave me his cell phone number, his friend's number in Los Angeles and his home phone number in New York. None of these came up as unavailable on caller ID.

This also brings up a revers point. My friends and I have dubbed it "When celebrities stalk back." Both Roger and Nick exhibited traits that at times got a bit creepy as far as I was concerned.

Roger called me when he received the first letter. He did not hesitate to give me his home number. He didn't just return my calls, he called me to see how I was. He told me about his life and his kids. He was extremely open. We had conversations that lasted over an hour sometimes. He appeared to have no problem talking with a total stranger.

Nick was subtler. He received both letters. Several months after the second one he called. He had found it on his desk. He was intrigued. He gave me his pager number. We played phone tag for a few days. One Saturday I came home to see on my caller ID that he had called three times that day.

He called a lot. He called me from Los Angeles. He called me from New York. He called me from his cell phone. He called from home. He called from a friend's house. He called early. He called late.

This serves as a reminder that I wrote total strangers. I told them things about myself. I used a post office box but I did give out my home phone number. I opened myself up to them as they opened themselves up to me.

I didn't make it a habit of calling to harass these people. When they called it quits I abided by their decision (with one notable exception). I had chosen letters because they are less obtrusive. If a celebrity has chosen to end the contact, I respect that decision and do not call them.

I have acquired several home phone numbers as well as pager numbers. I did not abuse this trust that these celebrities have placed in me. I respect that it takes a lot for them to let down their guard enough to invite me into their homes and lives in such a manner. I was honored by such trust. It's encouraging to me that they wanted that kind of contact.

# Married vs. Single

The state of marriage is stable in Hollywood!  I did not receive responses from married men (with one notable exception).  Only a photo for a fan.  Wives, congratulate your husbands.

Sure, I received photos and autographs but not letters or phone calls from married men. The largest group of phone calls were from divorced men.  Boy did they want attention.  All of them were nice.  Two seemed much more interested in my breast size than my level of intelligence. Single men tended to lean toward the personal note.  One even sent a lovely card with a long note.  After I sent my photo, I never heard from him again.

Then there were the engaged men.  Engaged men were responsive and gracious.  I received two pictures with personal notes from men mere weeks before their wedding day.  Both had obviously read the letter as they referenced my letter. They seemed flattered and one was rather intrigued.  Both made it clear they were taken.  One responded with a personal letter to me. He was kind in his refusal of my attention.  Within a month he announced his engagement.  I sent them my wedding congratulations and wished them all the best in their married life.

# The Saga Ends

My friends and I discovered that Walt was to return to our town to play at our state fair. We got tickets and made plans to attend. I was so excited the day of the show, I hardly ate and couldn't think. I even blew off an industry networking event to attend the show.

Again, I sent flowers. Same flowers. Same message with my name and phone number. I bought a new pair of jeans. I wanted to look nice but casual. I rode with a couple of friends. We met more friends there. They brought some friends. It was a group of nine. The concert was free for general admission. We had reserved seats.

We needn't have worried about seating. There were a lot of empty seats. I thought this was odd for a free concert at a state fair on a Friday night. The show wasn't as good as before either. There was feedback with the sound. The staging was bland. The stage crew could be seen wandering about behind the stage. The energy was lower overall. Walt also looked tired.

Before the show, I went down front and asked a security person how I checked the backstage list. She didn't know. She called another guy on the radio. He came out and had a list for a meet and greet after the show. I wasn't on it. I sent a note back with my name and message "Did you like the flowers this time?" I returned to my seat and watched the show.

After the show, I headed to where I saw others going backstage. The security stopped me. I asked about a backstage list. They said I needed a badge and sticker. I asked where the list was to see who was supposed to have those badges. They told me I needed a badge. It seemed as if that was what they were told and that was all they knew. No one told me where the backstage door was or tried to help me in any way. I had asked others and they didn't even seem to have ever heard the words "backstage list."

My friends were kind and understanding. I cried a bit on the ride home. It was a big letdown. I checked my machine upon returning home. He didn't call. Luckily there wasn't a chocolate cake in the house. It would have ceased to exist that night. I cried into my pillow and vowed not to let his rejection depress me. No eating every chemically enhanced food known to man. No going to the store and buying everything on the shelves. No locking myself in my home and watching black and white romantic movies (not even the color ones). Eleanor Roosevelt said it best when she said that no one can make you feel bad without your consent. He did not have my consent.

Perhaps he never got my flowers. They may have been delivered to the fairgrounds and never made it to Walt. I may have been on a list along with crew and staff but the people I asked didn't have any idea about that. I don't know. I probably never will.

I sent him a card. It provided closure.

"I attended the concert at the fair. It was very good, but I didn't expect anything less. I hope you received the flowers I sent. I hope they made you smile.

I checked before and after the show with security. I was sorry to learn I was not on the backstage list. I would have liked to say hello.

My best wished go to you with this card. If you ever need or want a friend or another fan, let me know. I'll be here."

So, life goes on. The world goes 'round. And Walt does not get to be as happy as I would have made him. Upon hearing that I was completely ignored by Walt at this show, the declaration was the same from my friends. "Maybe he's gay." Maybe he is. Maybe he's not. Maybe I'll never know. Maybe what happened at the first show was an elaborate way to appease a fan.

If he's not gay he missed the best thing that could have happened to him. Poor Walt.

# The Closet Door

As I made no distinction to age, race or marital status for those men who received the letter, I also made no concession as to sexual orientation.

Some men are open about their homosexuality while others hide it from the public to protect their image and thus their careers. There are rumors of course. Being in the entertainment industry, I am privy to knowledge that does not reach the press.

I did not receive a single positive response from any man who is gay or even suspected of being so. This was a good thing. As my letter was seeking a heterosexual relationship of a romantic nature, any man that is gay should not have responded. Why encourage the attention? Of those that I believe to have no interest in me because I am a woman, I only received a photo from one and a letter of flattery but a refusal of my attention from another.

I may have received another response or two from a gay man. If I have, they are hiding their orientation from the world. If they are happy that way, fine. I wish them well.

# The Last Letter to Walt

I am so glad that I met you. Knowing you will be a shining memory in my life. I realize that this will most likely be the last time I write you. I wish you had given me a chance. I may never know why you chose not to get to know me. Maybe a bit of shyness and insecurity. Maybe a lack of attraction. A friend suggested that maybe I was intimidating. I doubt that. I'd like to share some things I feel since this is my last chance.

I have come to truly believe in love at first sight. No man has ever affected me as you did. At the time I met you, I had three men who wanted to marry me. One had been proposing for five years. One of the oddities of my life is that men propose to me on a regular basis. I have had twenty-one men suggest marriage to me. Twelve of those have been formal proposals. Several have presented rings. I knew that none of them was right for me. Then I met you.

My life changed in fifteen minutes. I am currently not dating anyone. I haven't for some time. No man holds interest for me. After I met you, I wrote my best friend and told he "take me to the checkout stand because I'm done shopping." Men I had been attracted to before are now merely men I know. I don't want to know them on a romantic level. I don't want to know any man on a romantic level except you.

I wish I was capable of putting into words what I feel. I am normally very eloquent especially with the written word. My brain gets all muddled with you. I know I came across as a blathering idiot when we met. Not the example of a woman who was an honors student and a repeated member of the dean's list in college. I read text books for fun. If I hadn't chosen to go into film, I would have pursued a career in science. I considered getting a PhD in marine biology, specializing in cetaceans (primarily humpback whales but also blues and greys). I have a poster of Albert Einstein in my apartment. The quote says "I want to know God's thoughts. The rest are details." This is true of me.

I digress and I apologize. From the first moment that I looked into your eyes, I was lost. I had often heard stories of people who met and they knew in that instant they had found the one for them. One of these stories came from my parents. The met and within two months they were married. I am a highly sensible woman. I had come to accept the fact that I might never meet a man that I would consider right for me. I wondered if a man existed that possessed intelligence, a sense of humor, a love of music and good looks. Then I met you.

With my friends, I looked up information on the web and watched interviews. They agreed you were perfect for me. That we match in every way. I do not drink alcohol at all, I do not smoke, I have never done drugs and people apologize when they swear around me.

My true vice is chocolate. I love to read trashy romance novels. I bite my nails. I enjoy fairs, amusement parks and carnivals. I absolutely love circuses. I have entered three "beauty" pageants but never won. I used to model. I was even a bikini model on occasion. I listen to music constantly. I sing and dance at home. I have a great garden.

The moment you looked at me I felt as if you could read what was written on my soul. I was filled with joy surrounded by a cloud of serenity. I thought of what I could do and be for you not what you could do for me. I wanted to support you in any way I could. I was concerned for you during the tour for both your physical and emotional safety. I hoped you were getting enough rest. I wanted to do whatever I could to make you happy. I now realize that that may mean leaving you alone.

I wish you had felt even half of what I felt. I wish I had kissed you. I wish you had asked me to go with you that night. I wish I could have spoken with you at the second show. I wish you peace, joy and love in your life. If you ever need a friend, I will be there for you. You can trust me with anything, including your heart. Please take care of mine as I gave it to your when we met. I love you.

# Picture This

One of the most common requests I received was for a picture. Either it was to be assured that I did not have the look of a psychotic axe murderer or merely a testament to the shallowness of men. When asked I was happy to oblige. Unfortunately, upon sending a photo of myself, I often did not receive any further communications. As I see myself in the mirror each day, I know I do not look like a crazed killer. So, one must assume that my unique look does not appeal to a large segment of the male population.

This situation felt similar to that of mail order brides of the past. If she doesn't look good, don't send her the train ticket west to marry you. I received no train tickets.

It is sad to think that men are only interested in the superficial. Celebrities are often paid for their appearance, so it is only natural that they place a high value on looks. It would also seem to fit that they understand the lack of depth involved in such judgements. In knowing this, they should look beyond a woman's physical attributes to find inner qualities to appreciate.

# Mixed Signals

A lot of changes occurred during this process. One such change was that I obtained a computer and could look up things in the internet. (Yes, it took me a long time to finish this book). This has helped with research and also brought me some unexpected news. Actually, unwanted news as well.

Walt is not gay. That's the good news. The bad news (for me at least) is that less than 11 months after we met, he married someone else. It could have been a really fast thing. Granted I would have considered changing my entire life if he had asked me. My bad luck is that he asked someone else.

I would like to think that if he had been seriously involved with another woman, he should not have been meeting me in his dressing room alone. I had sent a letter clearly stating my attraction (okay, so it was a form letter). And had sent flowers to him. If he was at a point in a relationship where he would get married within a year, he really should not have been meeting women in his dressing room.

He did not mention a girlfriend. When I asked if he wanted to keep in touch, he said yes. He seemed genuinely pleased to meet me and not as a mere fan.

I have dated my fair share of men. Maybe more than my fair share. I have had numerous men declare their love and quite a few propose. I have learned to recognize that look in a man's eyes. I know that I am not unattractive. I am fairly intelligent and friendly. I was looked at as a woman by him, not as a fan.

Walt seemed nervous and fidgety as we spoke. Perhaps he knew it was not the proper thing to be doing. What if his girlfriend/fiancé found out he was meeting women in his dressing room while on tour. I felt that I would not be too understanding if I were to learn that the man I was seriously involved with met with a woman who had written him on several occasions to express her interest in him as a man, not a performer. Then to call her several times and put her on the backstage list when performing in her town. That is beyond the standard kindness towards a mere fan. Those are the actions of a man towards a woman.

I suppose that when he hugged me (his idea) and agreed to keep in touch (my idea), that fact of a woman in his life slipped his mind. Hopefully, for her sake, his memory will be better in the future. Perhaps I was lucky that he did not pursue me if this is his standard behavior when involved.

Another option, and the one I wish to believe, is that I helped him make the final decision that she was the right one. When I called him at the studio, the man that answered sked if I was (insert woman's name here). That is the woman he married. Maybe he was sure of her but needed to meet me face to face out of curiosity and so he wouldn't always wonder if I was the one. When he met me, he was sure she was the right one.

Whatever the reason, I wish him the best of luck in his marriage. I hope she is patient and kind and, above all, understanding. I have learned that there are good honest men as well as those that forget they are involved, engaged or married. Walt is not the only one to be forgetful. I am sure he won't be the last. Men are men no matter the career or level of fame. As women, we must look carefully to find the good ones. Hopefully we won't be hurt too much by the not so good ones. Then we can make the good ones very happy and fully loved. That is what Walt missed out on with me.

# Child Stars

Stop. Don't get the wrong idea from that title. I did not write children. The men I sent letters to were all legal adults. I did write several that had been child stars. The men I chose were on television series. They had been picked for their cute charm.

I've noticed that these boys with their apple cheeks often grow into men with apple cheeks. I received autographed photos from several. Then, there was Ted.

Ted did not respond to the first letter so he received the second letter. I got a response from that one. Actually, I received my letter back with notes in the margin. When I wrote I had an attractive figure, he underlined it and wrote "show me". When I wrote of what I did not have as far as material possessions, he wrote "no prob." At the end of the letter, he said he would like detailed pictures. Also, I should mark my photos "private."

It had a rather disturbing air about it. Ted had played on a family show where he was the good child. Basically, the standard role for male child stars. Now he was asking for "detailed" pictures of me sent to him and marked "private". What kind of pictures did he want?

I thought a lot about the options and finally decided to send a photo. I sent him the same photo that I had sent everyone else. It is a nice photo of me in a short tight black dress. It was taken when I was in my mid-twenties. I included a note that I would like to get to know him better. He could write or call anytime. He never did.

This goes to prove the difference that age makes as well as the dissimilarity between the roles an actor plays and the actor himself. What we see on the screen is often very different from who that person really is. Fans are often surprised when they hear that their favorite clean cut wholesome actor was arrested for drug possession or spousal abuse. They are playing a role and often it is easiest to play a character completely opposite from your own personality.

I have since learned that Ted is married and has kids. He is in his mid-50s, has brown hair and had a successful television show.

# The One I Let Get Away

"I don't know if I would follow him down the street panting, but he is nice looking." This is how I chose to describe one that was not written. He is one that I let get away. There was no spark whatsoever from either of us. It was flat and dull.

He was in his mid-50s, divorced and has a child. He lives in Los Angeles. He has had a successful television career. He has dark hair.

We met through work. I received only a brief glance upon introduction. Maybe he didn't like my tight, low-cut top. Perhaps he didn't appreciate my ethnic look. Maybe he has no taste. Everyone else on the set spoke of how nice he was. Maybe a work situation was not the best atmosphere in which to meet. Either way, I felt about as much attraction as I do toward a piece of furniture. An average piece of furniture, nothing too fancy or high quality.

One thing that annoyed me was his reference to me as "sweetheart." "Thank you, sweetheart." "See you later, sweetheart." "Take care, sweetheart." Since this was a professional atmosphere and he was obviously not bowled over by my stunning beauty, I can only surmise that he referred to me as sweetheart because he didn't bother to pay attention to what my name was. He heard others call me by name. I was introduced by name. Yet I was only "sweetheart." Celebrity does not mean depth of character or manners.

If I were to meet him again and he made romantic advances toward me, I would have to say, "Sorry, sweetheart."

# Moving On

Surprisingly, I bounced back from the entire Walt experience fairly quickly. I was still having men occasionally calling me. I was still getting letters. I got fan club information and form letters. And the pictures were still coming. I was added to a mailing list to keep me up to date on one actor's every role.

I began to think back on all the really interesting men that had contacted me and I smiled a lot. One stayed in my mind longer than the others. One that I had had an interest in before all this began. Brian.

Even though I had let the contact stop because of him not being comfortable with the age difference, I missed talking with him. I decided to break a policy I was trying to follow and contact him.

I wrote him a brief note explaining that I missed our talks and hoped he was well. He was free to contact me if he wanted to. I would leave it up to him. We were both older. Several years had passed by this point. (Yes, this process went on for a long time).

I mailed the letter and waited. I hoped but didn't expect anything.

# Signature Required

I received many photos in response to my letter. Often they had only a preprinted signature. Occasionally they had a real signature. Then there were the ones that had my name and a salutation of some sort.

Those that had a brief message were the best. They had a more personal feel. I felt as if my letter had actually been read by the person to whom it was sent and they responded.

You can tell a lot about a celebrity by how they respond to a letter. There are some that are overrun with fan mail and cannot possibly respond to each letter. These are the ones that have preprinted signatures on their photos. They are mailed in mass to those people who send fan letters. Often they are sent from one of the celebrity fan mail processing centers. These companies handle fan mail responses for many celebrities. They mail photos to people who write letters. From the responses I received, I don't believe they even read the letters but merely copy the address off the letter onto an envelope. Then they include the appropriate photo of who the letter was addressed to and mail it. The photos are metered so it is obvious that they handle mass mailings.

I was sent a few photos that had the address portion of my letter cut out and taped onto the envelope. I would have liked someone to at least bother to write or type my name. One such photo was a postcard. My name and address were cut from my letter and taped to the card. It was done in such a haphazard way that placed my address near the stamp at an angle. This postcard came from an actor that is very popular with teenage girls. I am sure he gets a lot of mail but this was just sloppy.

Handwriting can be compared easily. Often the envelope is written by one person. The photo is signed by the celebrity and the additions are added later by someone else. It has an assembly line feel. The celebrity may sign a large quantity of photos at once. Then another person will add my name and personalize it. Yet another is in charge of addressing the envelopes. There were many times the ink color changes. Feminine handwriting addressing envelopes of male stars.

All these small details show what care and amount of time celebrity spends in dealing with his fans. Many truly don't have any spare time to handle all their mail. That is why they hire assistants or fan mail companies. This is understandable but adds a feeling of apathy from the celebrity.

I truly appreciate those men that actually responded with a personalized photo. Those that sent notes were interesting. Those that called were adventurous. The ones that sent flat boring photos or had an outside company handle their mail for them missed out on reading my letter. The cross-section of responses was enlightening.

I proved this point to myself by bordering on stalking. I set the letter to a popular television star. Nice looking guy. Single, no kids. He has dark hair and is close in age to me.

I got a photo with a preprinted signature from a fan mail company. I wrote back and thanked him for the photo. I got another photo. Well, actually the same photo again. Same fan mail company. I wrote again. I got another copy of the photo. I kept this going for months. I probably have six to eight copies of this same photo of this actor. I was sending senseless notes about my day to him and I would get a photo from the fan mail company. I decided to stop because I was sure I was due a restraining order if they ever looked at their records. But I did learn that many actors are very detached from their fans.

# The Return of Brian

I mailed my letter to Brian and figured I would have a long wait if he replied at all. It would take a few days to even get to him. Three days from the day I mailed my letter, he called.

He was thrilled to hear from me and really wanted to talk and catch up but he was heading out of the country for a couple weeks. He said he would call me when he got back. Two weeks later he called me back. He again told me he was glad I had written. We had a long conversation to catch up. I didn't realize how much I missed talking with him until we got back in touch.

It seemed as though he missed me too. I was welcome to call him anytime I wanted. He called me too. We quickly were talking two to three times a week. Our conversations were often an hour and many times more than that.

We caught each other up on what had been happening in our lives. Our conversations were deeper than they had been previously. Any issues he had with our difference in ages were gone. He opened up more to me than he had before. We shared. We grew closer and closer.

# Handwriting

Sometimes a personalization on a photo can cause problems. An actor I received a photo from had signed it himself. The only problem was that it looked like he wrote "all my lust." This confused me. I showed it to my friends and they said it looked like it said "all my lust."

I wrote him back and thanked him for the photo but was unsure what I should do with all his lust. We didn't know each other after all. I soon got a different picture of him with "all my BEST" printed not in cursive as before. This clarified the confusion for me. I hope he was amused by my response.

Neatness matters. This could have gotten out of hand easily. He is a nice looking man, but in this situation I prefer all his best.

# Email

I had a very busy schedule and so did Brian. We implemented email into our communication. This helped us touch base if we couldn't talk on the phone. He traveled a lot and we could reach each other this way without worry about time zones or who was around.

Some of these helped break down barriers. I told him once that I had purchased a cordless phone. This would make it easier to talk in bed. His response was to ask me if we needed a phone to talk in bed. Yes, our relationship had progressed beyond fan and actor when we first started talking. Now, we were taking that relationship further.

Maybe it was easier to take that step through a computer. Safety of electronica.

Of course we still lived hundreds of miles apart and had never met face to face. So it was still in a fantasy realm of sorts.

# Stats

I tried to see if there were any patterns to the answers I got. I created charts and graphs. I researched every detail about those celebrities that responded to see if I could find a pattern.

First I looked at age. Older stars were more likely to respond than the younger generation. The strongest level of communication including phone calls was from men in their mid-50s. Specifically, divorced men with kids.

I checked to see of the stars had anything to do with it. I made lists of who fell into which sign of the zodiac. Well, that was a waste of time. They were all over the place.

And mentioning all over the place, birthplace may or may not have played a factor. A lot of men that were born in the Midwest responded in some way. There also seemed to be a heavy representation from Pennsylvania.

I then checked into religion. Most of the responses came from Christian men. And among those it was a cross section of denominations. No one specific religious representation stood out.

I searched for patterns. I tried to be very scientific to see if a certain type of man from a certain area would be more attune to their fans than others. Nothing clear was discovered. No matter where they came from or what they believed, how a celebrity relates to fans is entirely up to them.

# 9/11

It was a day all of us remember. A time when the country was suddenly thrown into some new form of itself. Where we felt all alone and together simultaneously. From that morning and throughout that day and those that followed, our lives and routines changed.

Planes were grounded. People stayed home. In the city it was eerily quiet. The sound of patrolling helicopters were the only thing that broke the silence and reminded us that there was someone looking out for us.

Thank goodness the phones worked. We all reached out to family and friends during those first few days. Brian and I reached out to each other. We discussed the horrible attacks, where our families were and that everyone was safe. Our conversations became deeper. Life was suddenly more precious.

In the days following 9/11, many of us reevaluated what was important. This wasn't a silly little pastime or entertaining anymore. It had value. Our relationship changed then. It became more real.

# Dinner

Just for fun I decided to send dinner invitations to a few of the celebrities that I wanted to meet but had not heard from. So, I wrote up a dinner invitation and sent them off.

I requested the honor of their presence at dinner. Naturally, the date, time and location was to be decided. I included my phone number as usual.

I only heard back from one man. I got a call from his office thanking me but due to the fact they were not quite sure who I was, they had to decline the invitation. He did leave a phone number. I called back and it was his office. I assumed it was an assistant that had called. I spoke to a very nice woman that informed me that it was indeed the actor himself that had called. She asked if I had met him somewhere and if that had prompted the invite. I was honest and told her no but I thought it would be a good way to get to know him. She was nice and got off the phone quickly. I am sure I was put on some list at that point.

It's a shame because he is a very talented actor and a good-looking man. I am sure we could have had a lovely dinner.

# Insecurities

When Brian and I reconnected, he did make a joke or two about my age. I said nothing about his. I know he felt odd about the difference in our ages. I think he wondered why I would be interested in him.

He is a talented, self-assured man. The only times that I see any crack in that confidence is when he wonders why I am attracted to him. Anyone who looks at the man would be attracted to him. Dark good looks and one of the sexiest voices I have ever heard is reason enough to be attracted.

Over time I have gone beyond the physical attractiveness of him. We have talked about his life and mine. He tells me about his children and his work. He is proud of his family and a concerned father.

We like the same music and enjoy travel. We talk and laugh about many things. He is cultured and educated. Looks can fade but intelligence and a kind heart last. He has these and more.

One thing about me that bothers him is that we don't talk often enough. I am very slow about returning calls. He wants to talk to me more. He wants to meet me face to face.

# Athletes

One group that I have not discussed too much is athletes. I have talked mainly about actors as they were the largest group written and the largest response as well with photos and more.

Musicians came next with mainly fan club information but also photos and letters. All very polite and professional. The odd exception was the letter from a musician who referred to himself in the third person.

Athletes rarely responded. I heard back from two even though I had written many more than that. One was a polite letter of thanks but he was not interested. The other was a very friendly postcard with a note.

I am not sure why athletes don't relate to their fans the same s actors or musicians. Perhaps it is personality or they see their jobs differently.

# Am I In A Relationship?

The interest Brian has shown me goes beyond a celebrity who is curious about a fan. We have reached the point of a man and a woman getting to know each other. A man and a woman who are interested in one another.

One morning he phoned me at a rather early hour. It was 6:45am for him. He never identified himself to me, merely assumed (correctly) that I would recognize his voice. He was getting the kids ready for school. He called to let me know he was thinking about me. That was all. It shocked me that he would be thinking of me at such an hour or while doing routine family activities. However, it is not unusual for me to think of him often. He will pop into my mind while I am doing the most mundane things.

During one of our phone calls, he did a simple yet extraordinary thing. He called me "sweetie." This is now a common endearment from him. I am not one that is given to endearments so I have not applied one to him yet.

When he calls me sweetie I smile and feel closer to him. I am also glad that he feels comfortable with me to the level of calling me by a pet name.

I look forward to our phone calls. I smile after they have ended.

# Tis The Season

As the holidays approached, I did my normal decorating and enjoying the season. I sent Brian a book I found that I knew he would enjoy. He was truly surprised by it.

He surprised me more. One night as we were talking, he asked if I wanted to spend Christmas with he and his kids at a ski area where they were spending the holidays. This caught me off guard. He and I had never even been in the same room and now he was asking me to spend one of the biggest holidays of the year with his family.

I told him I couldn't. I had plans with my family already. I also thought it would be very awkward getting to know him with his kids around. It would definitely be strange for them. He understood.

A couple days later as we were talking, he suggested I come stay with him as the same ski area for New Year's. The kids would have gone home to their mom and so he and I could spend time alone together. He promised I would have my own room and everything. No pressure.

Well, this was different. I had the clothes for snowy weather. I had enough time that I could take off work. I had the means to fly there. I really wanted to go. But then my rational mind started doing that pesky thing it does.

I realized how absolutely crazy it would be for me to agree to spend several days alone with a man I had only spoken to on the phone. True we had logged a lot of hours into what we had, but being around someone is different. I knew if I went there, I would be very vulnerable too.

Phone calls and closeness are one thing. Being with someone 24 hours a day all alone is a whole different experience. That was something I would rather build up to not jump right into. I told him no. He said he understood although he was disappointed.

# RIP

From the time that this process began until now years later, a number of the men that I had written have passed away. I have pictures and notes from some. I can remember them whenever I see them on television or in the movies.

I know it will be sad when those I spoke with or got a personal note from leave us. This entire process has changed the line of them and me. I feel a closer connection to some performers because of this. They are no longer just celebrities but individuals.

# On Tour

One aspect of Brian's job as an actor was in theatre. He performed on stage regularly. We would talk or email when he was on the road if his schedule permitted. I wanted him to know I was thinking about him during this time. Our normal routine was different when he wasn't at home.

I got his touring schedule. Then I arranged for flowers to be in his dressing room on opening night at each venue. It was a special way to let him know I was thinking of him.

As I studied the show dates and locations, I saw that one was in a nice locale and not too far. I spoke with a couple of my friends and they agreed to my plan. I was going to attend his show.

We made hotel reservations. We bought tickets. I bought a very sexy dress. We were all set to go. Only one thing I did not do. I did not tell Brian I was coming.

The evening of the play, we found the theatre early. In fact, we were passing it just as Brian was getting out of his car to go in. This was the first time I had ever seen him in reality. My friends asked if I wanted to stop to say hello. I said no. I did not want to mess up his pre-curtain routine or have him know I was in the audience. But he looked great. He moved so smoothly.

The play was incredible. We loved it as did the rest of the audience. After the show, there was a reception nearby. We attended.

I'm sure Brian had noticed he did not receive his usual flowers. The idea was that I was the flowers instead. I was so nervous at the reception that I actually sat and just watched him for a long time. It gave me a chance to reconcile that I was actually there near him. This man that I had had a crush on as a girl. This man whose talent I had admired for so long. This man that I had come to know deeply and felt close to.

At one point I went to the rest room. As I was walking back to my table, I saw Brian watching me. More than watching. His eyes traveled up my body. From my high heeled shoes past my short hemline over my clingy dress and finally to my face. When he saw that I saw him checking me out, he quickly looked away. He was all man but also a gentleman. He also seemed a bit embarrassed that he had been caught.

He was speaking with someone so I walked past him and back to my table. When he finally ended that conversation, I made my move. I walked up to him and told him I really enjoyed the show and he did a wonderful job. He started out with one expression of politeness which then changed as I was speaking. Recognition dawned with the sound of my voice and he asked "Is this you?" I said yes and he immediately embraced me and kissed my cheek.

He held my hand for a bit then released it as I introduced my friends to him. We chatted for a bit casually. There were a number of people around that needed his attention.

My friends and I left to return where we were staying. Brian and his friends left at the same time. As we drove away I watched Brian. He had what I can only describe as an expression of longing on his face. Almost as though he wished he could go with me.

It was a magical time. Dreams do come true sometimes.

After my return home, our talks and emails intensified. Now we had a physical image and sense to put to all our thoughts. He was still very busy but we made time to stay in touch.

# Reality

My life did continue on during all of this. I had work and friends and even dates. Brian and I had made no declarations to each other or talked of what we had or where we thought it was going. It was very much in the moment.

One day a friend from high school and I met for lunch. We ended up talking for 3 hours. We met again and again. Then we started talking on the phone.

It is really strange how life takes its twists and turns. Some totally unexpected things can happen that we were not looking for at the time.

I was still talking with Brian but it shifted to mostly emails. In one e-mail I told him I was happy to have such a special friend. He asked why he was regulated to a "special friend". He knew things had changed. I knew it too.

Whereas my emotions for Walt hit me like a thunderbolt, my feelings for Brian were a warm summer rain. Soft and gentle. You are in it and don't realize what is happening until you are drenched and you find yourself smiling with the joy of the situation.

But thunder and rain need two major things; air and ground. I had neither of these with Walt or Brian. I could not breathe normally with them. I never felt as though I was on solid footing either. For a true relationship, you need that.

I found that in the real world. A man that gave me air to breathe and stretch while at the same time keeping my feet firmly planted on the ground. Like a tree this is what we need to truly grow. Of course I said yes when he asked me to marry him.

Brian said we could still be friends but I knew it was not the right thing to do. What we had had run its course. My life was based in reality. I had lived my fantasy. I would always have fond happy memories.

A woman can reach for the stars in love but every astronaut has to return to earth at some point. My feet are now on solid ground.

# Conclusion

Once a celebrity has touched your life, you are somehow changed. It may be involved in all the mysticism that surrounds their life. It may be the fact that at any moment you might catch a glimpse of that person on television or in a movie. To hear them on the radio or read an article in a magazine you happen to pick up.

After several years of this celebrity involvement and writing, I know I can see them at any time. I've seen men I know on "Biography" or "Behind the Music." They are there if I read celebrity magazines or watch entertainment shows.

I laugh to myself when I see one of the idiots acting in the egotistical manner I have seen firsthand. I am please when one of them finds love and gets married. I am sorry when someone cannot find work and drifts into the world of the has-been. Then there are those that I miss speaking with or would have enjoyed the chance to know better.

No matter what the circumstance of the meeting, contact or involvement, I enjoy seeing someone I have crossed lives with, however briefly, and I smile.

# About the Author

Traci E. Langston lives quietly with her husband and cats. They lead normal lives as she continues to write a variety of books. While keeping feet firmly planted, she still dreams of doing great things.

Made in the USA
San Bernardino, CA
03 March 2020